DESERTS

Written by **Jenny Wood**

Consultant Roger Hammond
Director of Living Earth

Scholastic Canada Ltd

123 Newkirk Road, Richmond Hill (Ontario) Canada

DESERTS

Copyright © Two-Can Publishing Ltd., 1991
Text copyright © Jenny Wood, 1991
Design by Claire Legemah
Edited by Claire Watts

First published in Great Britain in 1991 by
Two-Can Publishing Ltd
27 Cowper Street
London WC2A 4AP

Published in Canada in 1992 by
Scholastic Canada Ltd.
123 Newkirk Road
Richmond Hill, Ontario
Canada L4C 3G5.

Printed and bound in Hong Kong

Canadian Cataloguing in Publication Data
Wood, Jenny
Deserts

Canadian ed.
Includes index.
ISBN 0-590-74364-3

1. Deserts - Juvenile literature. I. Title.

GB612. W66 1992   j508.315'4   C92-093308-4

Photographic Credits:
Cover (front) Tony Stone (back) Bruce Coleman; p. 5 Bruce Coleman; p. 6/7 Frank Lane; p. 8 (top) Frank Lane (bottom) Survival Anglia; p. 9 Planet
Earth Pictures; P. 10 Ardea; p. 10/11 Zefa; p. 12/13 Graham Robertson; p. 14 (top) Survival Anglia (bottom) Robert Harding; p. 15 Survival Anglia;
p. 16 Bruce Coleman; p. 17 Ardea; p. 18 (top) Bruce Coleman (bottom) Bruce Coleman; p. 19 Hutchison; p. 20 Ardea; p. 22 (top) Sygma (bottom) Bruce
Coleman; p. 23 Robert Harding.

Illustrations Credits:
All illustrations by Francis Mosley except p. 24-28 Jon Davis/Linden Artists.

CONTENTS

All words marked in **bold** can be found in the glossary

WHAT ARE DESERTS?

If you were asked to describe a desert, you would probably think of these three words: hot, dry and sandy. But it is not as simple as that. Most of the world's deserts are in warm regions, but others, such as the Gobi Desert in Asia, can be extremely cold. In winter, temperatures there can reach as low as -12° C. The areas around the North and South Poles are classed as deserts, too, and they are most certainly cold.

All deserts are dry. They receive less than 25 cm of rain or snow each year. But desert landscapes include gravel, boulders and mountains. Sand covers only about ten percent of most desert areas.

▶ Sand dunes in the Namib Desert of south-west Africa.

▼ The world's main deserts. Although many scientists use the amount of annual rainfall to classify an area as a desert, others examine the type of soil and **vegetation**.

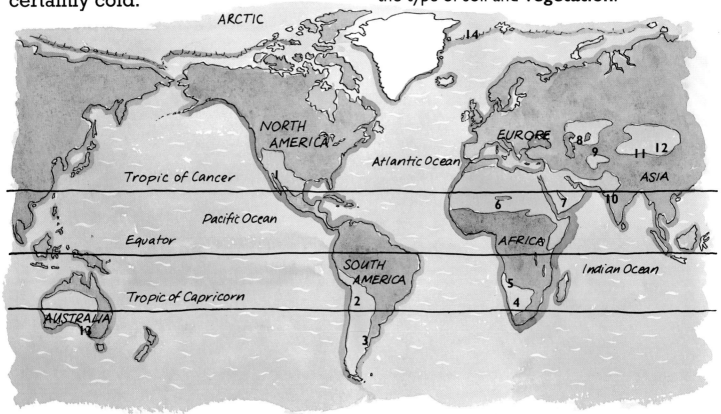

1	Great Basin (includes Death Valley, Mojave, Sonora and Chihuahua Deserts)	2	Atacama Desert	7	Arabian Desert	12	Gobi Desert
		3	Patagonian Desert	8	Kara Kum	13	Australian Desert
		4	Kalahari Desert	9	Kyzyl Kum	14	North Pole
		5	Namib Desert	10	Thar Desert	15	South Pole
		6	Sahara	11	Taklimakan Desert		

HOW DESERTS ARE FORMED

Most deserts are located near the equator, in areas known as the tropics. As warm air flows from the equator toward the tropics, it rises and cools. As the air cools, it releases its moisture as rain. By the time it reaches the tropics, the air is beginning to move down toward the land and warm up again. This warm air soaks up all the moisture in the ground below, and a dry desert area is created. The Sahara in Africa is a tropical desert.

DID YOU KNOW?

● The only regular supply of moisture to the Namib Desert is the fog that rolls in from the cold South Atlantic Ocean every day. Some creatures have developed ways of using this moisture. One beetle stands upside down with its back to the incoming fog and allows moisture to condense on its body. It then catches the water droplets as they trickle along its back towards its mouth.

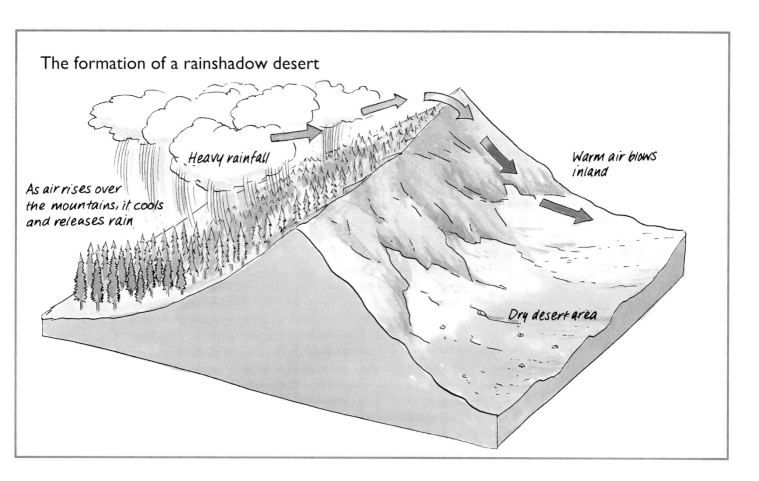

The formation of a rainshadow desert

Heavy rainfall

As air rises over the mountains, it cools and releases rain

Warm air blows inland

Dry desert area

Some deserts, such as the Taklimakan Desert in China, lie in areas which are separated from the sea by mountains. Here, a type of desert known as a rainshadow desert is created.

Coastal deserts, such as the Namib Desert in southwest Africa, lie near the sea. Air masses move across the cold ocean and lose their moisture before reaching land.

Some deserts, such as the Gobi Desert and the Gibson Desert, are found in places far inland where the air is hot and dry.

◀ When rain falls in a desert, it usually comes as a sudden downpour. Water may collect in channels or dry lake beds.

SAND, ROCK AND SALT

The appearance of deserts varies a great deal. High mountains, huge, shifting sand dunes, vast expanses of stony ground and huge boulders are all found in different deserts throughout the world. Some deserts include all these different types of landscape. Desert areas like Death Valley in the USA have dried-up lake beds which are covered in a layer of glistening salt. Areas such as Antarctica are completely covered in a thick sheet of ice.

▲ If floodwaters pouring down from surrounding hills cannot flow away, they become trapped in the desert valley and form a lake. As the lake dries out, it leaves a layer of salt. The layers of salt build up, until the whole area becomes a **salt pan**.

◀ Sometimes all sand is blown away from a desert area, leaving only bare rocks.

▶ The tallest of the rock formations in Monument Valley, Arizona, USA, rise as high as 300 m. The landscape has been worn away over thousands of years, to form flat-topped hills known as **mesas** and columns of rock called **buttes**.

HOT DESERTS

The Sahara is the world's largest hot desert. It stretches right across the north of Africa from the Atlantic Ocean in the west to the Red Sea in the east. Altogether, the Sahara covers about 9 million km^2.

During the last Ice Age, over 10,000 years ago, the Sahara had a much wetter climate and the region was covered with grasslands and forests. About 6,000 years ago, the climate in Africa became drier and gradually the Sahara began to turn into a desert.

▲ Dunes form as grains of sand are blown against obstacles and begin to pile up.

Scattered throughout the Sahara are fertile areas known as **oases**. Oases form in places where underground water flows to the surface or where there is a permanent river. The Sahara has about 90 large oases, where people live in villages and grow crops. Oases are a welcome sight to desert travellers.

Rain

Top of water table

Village with wells

Desert dunes

Oasis

Permeable rock allows water to pass through it

The Sahara is one of the hottest areas in the world. Temperatures of 58°C have been recorded there. Large areas of the eastern and western Sahara receive less than 2.5 cm of rain each year.

The landscape of the Sahara is very varied. Right in the centre, the high Ahaggar Mountains rise steeply. Northeast lies a region of rocky **plateaus** known as the Tassili. In the north and west of the Sahara are vast seas of sand called **ergs**. In some places, there are sand dunes 180 m high.

▼ The fertile green area around an oasis is a strange desert sight.

DID YOU KNOW?

● Sand is actually tiny pieces of rock and **minerals**, formed when larger rocks crumbled away.

● Sand dunes keep moving. Strong winds can move a dune about 30 cm in a day. Some towns and settlements on the edge of a desert become gradually covered with sand, forcing the people who live there to move.

● The toughest motor race in the world is considered to be the Paris-Dakar Rally. The course starts in Paris, France, and crosses much of the Sahara Desert to end in Dakar, Senegal. The total distance is over 10,000 km.

● Desert travellers sometimes see what they think is a pool of water in the distance. But when they reach the spot, they find only dry sand. The pool of water is a trick of light known as a **mirage**. A mirage occurs when a ray of light ripples as it passes first through cold air and then through warm air.

COLD DESERTS

Cold deserts are found in the world's polar regions, and on high mountains where the ground is frozen and there is little, if any, running water.

Antarctica is the coldest and iciest region in the world. A huge sheet of ice, 2,200 m thick, covers 98 percent of the continent. Much of the continent is a polar desert. Less than 5 cm of water falls each year, in the form of snow and ice crystals.

The temperature rarely rises above 0°C, and sometimes drops as low as -89°C.

You might think that nothing could live in this sort of climate. But tiny plant like creatures known as algae grow on the ice and snow.

Antarctica has no native human inhabitants, but about 900 scientists brave the Antarctic winters at science stations which have been set up there to study the ocean wildlife and the world's weather. The Arctic, on the other hand, is home to about 2 million people. Many Arctic lands have no snow and ice in summer, and Arctic people found ways of adapting to the cold.

Both the Arctic and the Antarctic are rich in mineral deposits. In the Arctic, oil, gold, copper and tin are mined. But in Antarctica, mining is forbidden for the time being. Many scientists are worried that large-scale mining would harm the **environment.**

KEEPING COOL

Animals that live in hot deserts have found ways of surviving in the hot, dry climate. Many of them move about at night, when it is cool. During the day, they shelter under rocks and plants, or in burrows. The animals that do move

▼ Camels are superbly adapted for life in the desert. They can travel for days without having to eat or drink. The fat contained in a camel's hump acts like a food store and provides the animal with the energy it needs.

▶ A sidewinder snake, its head half buried in the sand. Sidewinders move sideways across the sand, keeping most of their body clear of the ground.

◀ The Gila Monster is a type of lizard found in the deserts of the United States and Mexico. It is very slow-moving, but it has fangs like a snake and can kill prey with a **venomous** bite. The Gila Monster stores fat in its tail and can go for months without food.

around in the daytime heat often have ways of keeping their bodies away from the burning sand. The Saharan jerboa and the American kangaroo rat have long back legs to hop quickly over the ground. The frilled lizard of the Australian desert also runs on its back legs.

Creatures such as snakes and lizards, which are cold-blooded, need to warm themselves in the heat of the sun before they can move around. They hide in the shade when the sun is at its hottest. The main problem for desert animals is the lack of water. Some have found ways of storing water in their bodies. Others get all the moisture they need from the plants and insects they eat, and hardly ever need to drink at all.

Like many desert animals the fennec fox of the Sahara has large ears. These help the animal lose heat from its body and stay cool.

THE FLOWERING DESERT

Like desert animals, desert plants have also developed ways of making use of every drop of water. Some have long, tough roots, which burrow deep underground in search of moisture. The roots of the mesquite bush of the North American deserts go down as deep as 12 m below ground.

Many cacti have roots that spread over a wide area just below the surface of the ground. Water is carried up through the roots into the stem of the plant, which can store water.

Plants lose water through their leaves, so in dry desert areas many plants have tiny leaves that allow only a very small amount of water to escape. Others shed their leaves during long periods of no rainfall.

A number of plants simply do not grow at all during periods of **drought**. They lie as seeds in the soil, waiting for rain. When at last it does rain, the seeds **germinate** very quickly in the damp earth and, within a few days, the desert is a mass of colour.

DID YOU KNOW?

● Cacti can live for up to 200 years.

● The leaves of the desert holly grow almost vertically. This means that the fierce heat of the sun catches only the edges of the leaves, and so they lose very little moisture.

● As much as 80 percent of a giant saguaro cactus may be water.

● The stems of the jumping cactus plant break off very easily, and seem to jump on to any person or animal that passes by. The spines can cause painful wounds.

▶ The saguaro cactus stores water in its stem. After rain has fallen, cacti swell up as they fill up with water. They live on this stored water until the next rains come. Saguaros, found in the North American deserts, may reach a height of 18 m. In spring, flowers bloom on the tips of their branches and stems.

▼ The Kalahari desert in bloom after a rare period of rain. The flowers bloom for only a few days until the desert dries out again.

WIND, WATER AND HEAT

Although very little rain falls in desert areas, much of the shaping of the desert landscape is caused by water. When rain does fall, it is very heavy. The hard, dry soil cannot soak up the water, so it runs down slopes, forming **flash floods**. The water carves out steep-sided valleys know as **wadis**. Rocks, boulders and pebbles are carried

▶ This extraordinary boulder was created by wind and water **erosion**.

down from the valleys onto the desert plain.

Wind also helps to sculpture desert areas. Sand dunes are formed by wind, but sometimes the sand and soil are blown away completely, leaving bare rock surfaces known as rock pavements. Wind blows the sand with such force that any large rocks in its path are eroded.

Rocks on the surface of a desert are affected by heat, too. During the day they are heated, then at night, the rocks cool down. The constant heating and cooling weakens the rocks until eventually they crack.

▲ These eroded sandstone columns are in the Tessili plateaus of the Sahara.

◄ These badlands lie on the borders of Arizona and Utah in the USA. Badlands are barren areas of small, steep hills and deep valleys which have been worn away by wind and water.

Wadis are created by water rushing down desert slopes. They are dry for most of the year.

Flash floods rush downhill

Loose rocks, boulders and pebbles

Wadi

SURVIVING IN THE DESERT

The way of life of many desert peoples has changed in recent years. Many, such as the Bedouins of Arabia, used to be **nomads**. They had no permanent homes, but put up temporary shelters wherever they stopped. They lived by trading with other desert peoples, exchanging goods such as wool and leather for rice and grain. Their animals provided meat and milk, as well as wool and skin for clothing and tents.

Although some nomadic tribes still follow this traditional way of life, many have abandoned it. Some still spend part of each year travelling, but others now live in permanent campsites or oasis villages where they can grow crops. Others have moved to towns and cities in search of work.

One of the main reasons for these changing ways is that governments have made it more difficult for people to travel across borders between countries. Also, severe droughts have made it more difficult for people and animals to survive.

▼ Many Kurds, who live in an area of high mountains in Asia known as Kurdistan, are nomads. They live in tents and are skilled in breeding cattle, horses, sheep and goats.

CATCHING WATER

Desert travellers often make a **solar still** in order to catch water to drink. In hot weather, try making your own on a beach or in the garden, to see how it works.

You will need:
- A shovel
- A jar or can
- A sheet of plastic
- Stones

1 Dig a hole about 1 m across and 60 cm deep.

2 Place the jar or can in the centre of the hole.

3 Spread the sheet of plastic over the hole. Secure the edges with stones.

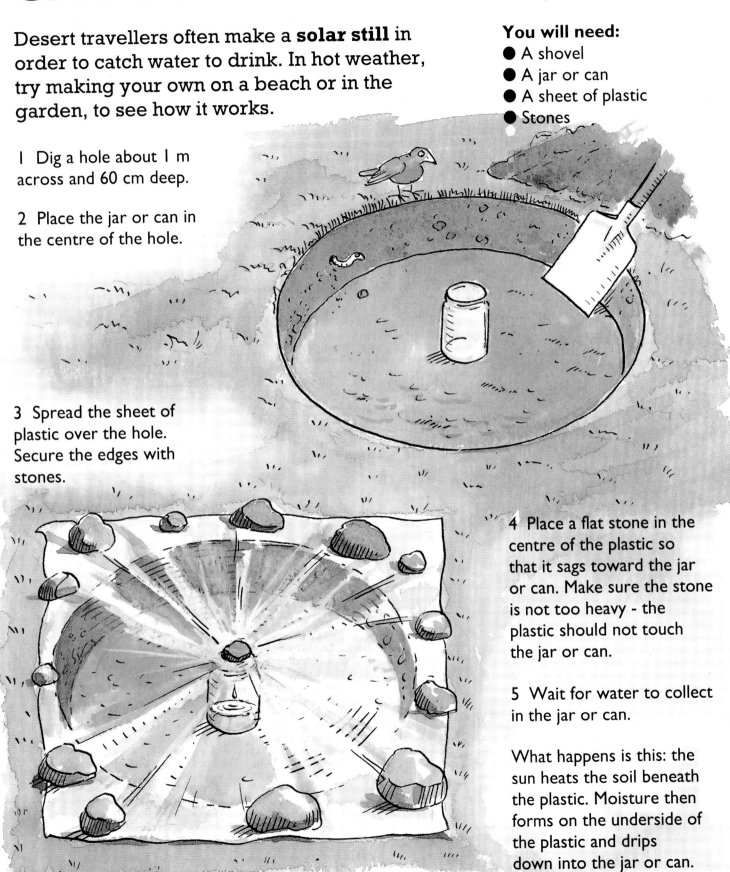

4 Place a flat stone in the centre of the plastic so that it sags toward the jar or can. Make sure the stone is not too heavy - the plastic should not touch the jar or can.

5 Wait for water to collect in the jar or can.

What happens is this: the sun heats the soil beneath the plastic. Moisture then forms on the underside of the plastic and drips down into the jar or can.

SCIENCE AT WORK

Desert lands are so dry that growing crops is difficult. Scientists have developed ways of watering the ground in some desert areas to make it fertile. Where there is water on the surface, a network of canals is built to carry water from the lake or river to the farmlands. Where water lies underground, wells are dug to pump the water to the surface. Watering desert lands in this way is known as **irrigation**.

Desert lands contain some of the world's most valuable mineral deposits. Diamonds are now mined in the Namib Desert in southwest Africa, and there are huge copper and **sodium nitrate** mines in the Atacama Desert in South America. Gold, uranium and aluminium have

▲ Each of these circular fields of wheat in Libya is watered by a long pipe on rails which rotates like the hands of a clock. The water is pumped up from underground.

◀ Narrow ditches called furrows carry water between rows of crops. The water flows through a pipe, and pours out through openings in the pipe into the furrows.

been discovered in the Australian Desert, and large quantities of oil and natural gas lie beneath parts of the Sahara, the Arabian Desert and the Great Basin.

Deserts receive a great deal of light and heat from the sun. Scientists have developed ways of capturing some of the **solar energy** in desert areas and turning it into electricity. Hundreds of flat or slightly curved mirrors are laid out over an area of desert land. The mirrors focus the sun's rays onto a target. A fluid is pumped through the target where it is heated. As the fluid warms up, it produces steam or gas, which then carries heat energy to turbines in a nearby power station that generate electricity.

▲ This open-pit copper mine lies in Arizona, USA. The copper-bearing rock is removed from horizontal layers called benches, which run up and around the sides of the pit.

DID YOU KNOW?

● Deserts are on the move. Each year, many of the world's deserts increase in size. One of the main reasons for this is that fertile land along the edges of the deserts is being made barren by cattle and other livestock that strip the ground bare of all its vegetation. Huge mining projects, as well as the destruction of trees, also have a part to play in this process which is known as desertification.

THE SEARCH FOR THE LOST CITY

Harry Philby could not remember when he had first heard the name Wabar. As soon as he heard the legend he decided that he would be the one to find the lost city. Storytellers told of the fabulous capital of King 'Ad Ibn Kin' ad which lay deep in the Rub' al Khali desert, with palaces encrusted with gems and surrounded by gardens bright with exotic flowers. Here, the king's glittering court had feasted and played, until at last the wrath of heaven had descended upon them, destroying the city with fire.

The city had been lost for 7,000 years. The river on whose banks it was supposed to have lain had long since vanished, covered over by the shifting desert sands. The

desert was known to the Arabs as 'the Empty Quarter'. They warned of the terrible dangers that lay within it. The sands, they said, were littered with the bleached skeletons of travellers and their

provisions. On the first night, as Philby stood by the campfire talking, he fainted. His face turned yellow, and his companions were convinced that he was going to die. They wrapped him up warmly and took turns to sit by him until morning. When he awoke, he felt perfectly well. The mystery illness had passed.

The expedition moved on. It seemed cursed with bad luck all the way. First the weather turned bitterly cold, so that the drinking water froze in the skins they carried. Then, a few days later it became unbearably hot. The line of camels trudged on through the sand. Grains of sand were whipped up all around them, turning their faces raw and getting into every crevice in their clothing.

camels who had perished in the burning heat.

But Philby was determined. On January 6, 1932, he set out with 18 men and 32 camels loaded with

Soon their water ran out. The Arabs spent much of the day searching for wells buried deep in the sand. When they found the wells, they had to spend hours digging before the water could be reached.

The party crossed the beds of two ancient dried-up rivers and eventually came to a third. This was, Philby believed, the river on which the city of Wabar had stood. At last, they camped within a day's journey of Wabar. Philby tossed and turned on his camp bed that night, haunted by dreams of the long-dead city.

The next day they marched on, following the river's course.

"Look!" shouted one of the guides suddenly.

Philby shaded his eyes against the glare of the sun. On the crest of a distant ridge, he saw what appeared to be a thin, low line of ruins.

He urged his camel on, thrilled by the prospect of turning his dream into reality. It took many hours to reach the top of the ridge

and the sky was darkening as Philby jumped down from his camel and ran forward across the sand to the wall.

He sank to his knees with a groan. He was looking down on the remains of an old volcano whose twin craters, encircled with low walls of rock and lava, were half-filled with drifting sand. He realized, with overwhelming disappointment, that the centuries-old legend still lay hidden beneath the shifting sands.

The next day his guides came to him and demanded that the expedition should leave. Philby, determined to get something out of the trip, ordered them to move on across 600 kilometres of burning, waterless desert.

They pressed on into the drought-stricken land. The rocks and sand seemed to vibrate with the heat. The camels became exhausted. The food and water had almost been used up. Even the Arabs had never seen such a desolate place. Then, on March 14, they emerged from the desert - the first people in history to cross the Empty Quarter from side to side.

TRUE OR FALSE?

Which of these facts are true and which ones are false?
If you have read this book carefully, you will know the answers.

1 Sand consists of tiny pieces of rocks and minerals.

2 All deserts are hot.

3 Most desert animals move about during the day.

4 The Sahara used to be covered with grasslands and forests.

5 Mesas and buttes are types of cacti.

6 Oases are fertile areas in a desert.

7 Sand covers half of all desert areas.

8 A mirage is a trick of light.

9 The temperature in a hot desert falls dramatically at night.

10 Rainshadow deserts lie on the coast.

11 Many desert peoples no longer follow a nomadic way of life.

12 Some desert plants store water in their stems.

GLOSSARY

Buttes are columns of rock in desert areas that have been worn away by wind, water and heat.

Drought is a long period of dry weather, with no rainfall at all.

Environment is a word used to describe a region that includes everything that affects it: its landscape, its human, animal and plant life, its weather and so on.

Ergs are huge areas of sand in the Sahara Desert.

Erosion is the gradual wearing away of the earth's surface.

Flash floods are sudden, violent floods that occur when rain falls in a desert. Because the ground is so hard and dry, the water cannot soak in and so rushes over the surface. The force of the water wears away the land.

Germinate means to start to grow and produce shoots.

Irrigation means building canals or digging wells to carry water to dry desert areas in order to make them suitable for growing crops.

Mesas are large, flat-topped hills. They are formed over thousands of years by the effects of wind, water and heat wearing away the rock.

Minerals are substances, other than plants, which can be dug from the ground.

Mirage is an optical illusion caused by heat. In the desert it often causes people to believe they see a pool of water in the distance.

Nomads are people who have no permanent home, but travel from place to place, building temporary shelters wherever they stop. Many nomads own herds of cattle, sheep or goats.

Oases are fertile areas in a desert, where underground water flows to the surface, or where there is a permanent river.

Plateaus are areas of high, level land.

Salt pans form when water dries out from a desert lake, leaving a layer of salt.

Sodium nitrate is used to make matches, explosives and fertilizers.

Solar energy is energy given off by the sun.

Solar still is a system of extracting water from the ground using the sun's heat.

Vegetation means the tree and plant life of a particular area.

Venomous means poisonous.

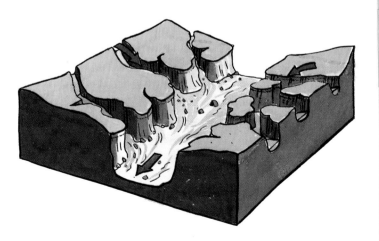

Wadis are steep-sided valleys in desert areas which have been carved out by water.

INDEX